Seahorses
Science Under The Sea

Lynn M. Stone

Rourke

Publishing LLC
Vero Beach, Florida 32964

www.rourkepublishing.com

PHOTO CREDITS: Cover, p. 4, 7 © James H. Carmichael; title page, p. 15 ©
Marty Snyderman; p. 8, 10, 12, 13, 16, 19, 20 © Brandon Cole.

Cover Photo: *A yellow seahorse from Brazil*

EDITOR: Frank Sloan

COVER DESIGN: Nicola Stratford

Library of Congress Cataloging-in-Publication Data

Stone, Lynn M.
 Sea horses / Lynn M. Stone.
     p. cm. — (Science under the sea)
Summary: Describes the physical characteristics, behavior, habitat, and
life cycle of these small but fierce predators.
Includes bibliographical references (p.   ).
 ISBN 1-58952-319-9 (hardcover)
 1. Sea horses—Juvenile literature. [1. Sea horses.] I. Title.
 QL638.S9 S77 2002
 597'.6798--dc21

                                            2002005131

Printed in the USA

CG/CG

Table of Contents

Seahorses

Animals aren't always what their names might make you think they are. You probably know that a prairie dog is a ground squirrel, not a dog. And a seahorse is not a horse, although it does live in the sea.

The head of a seahorse does have a curious likeness to a horse's head. But the seahorse is clearly a fish. Like almost all fish, it has fins, breathes through gills, and has a backbone.

Its head may be horse-like, but the seahorse is all fish.

An Unusual Fish

Still, the seahorse is a most unusual little fish. It has, of course, an unusual shape, and it swims upright. It has fewer fins than most fish. Its **dorsal** fin —the fin on its back—powers the seahorse along. That fin **flexes** up to 35 times per second!

The little dorsal fin provides horsepower for the seahorse.

The Seahorse's Tail

Unlike most fish, a seahorse has no scales. Its body is made up of bone sections called plates. The seahorse looks like it is wrapped in bony rings. Another unusual feature is the seahorse's tail. The tail can wrap around objects. The seahorse uses its tail to anchor itself onto sea grass and other **marine** plants.

A seahorse anchors itself by wrapping its tail around a hard coral branch.

Big and Small

The largest seahorse is the 1-foot- (.30-meter-) long Pacific. Many seahorses are less than 6 inches (15 centimeters) long. The smallest is an Australian seahorse under one inch (less than 2 centimeters).

At less than half an inch (10 millimeters) in length, this pygmy seahorse is one of the world's smallest seahorses.

*The Pacific seahorse of North America is the largest of the
32 kinds of seahorses.*

It's not seaweed but a leafy sea dragon, a close cousin of the seahorse.

Seahorse Habitats

Seahorses are fish of warm, shallow seas. They can be found, for example, in the shallow bays of the Florida coasts.

They like to hide in seagrass, on coral reefs, and among the roots of mangrove trees. Most of the more than 30 species of seahorses live in the western Atlantic and the warm waters of the Pacific and Indian oceans.

This seahorse blends in with the coral in which it's hiding.

Predator and Prey

Seahorses are small, but they are fierce **predators**. They eat only live animals, like small fish and **crustaceans** such as brine shrimp.

The seahorse has no teeth. It is a slurper. It sucks small **prey** into the narrow, round mouth at the tip of its snout.

A spotted seahorse shows the long snout that slurps prey.

Successful Predators

Seahorses are weak swimmers, yet they are successful predators. The secret is in **camouflage**. The seahorse is a master at hiding itself in its ocean home. A seahorse can actually change color to look like the plants around it. Some seahorses have long, spiky growths that help them look like seaweed.

With color to match its surroundings, a Pacific seahorse holds onto a sulfur sponge in Mexico.

Seahorse Parents

Seahorses are unusual parents. The female lays from dozens to hundreds of eggs into a pouch on the male seahorse.

The male carries the eggs from 10 to 45 days. Some species carry eggs longer than others.

When the eggs hatch, the male releases tiny baby seahorses into the ocean.

This plump male seahorse has a belly pouch full of seahorse babies.

A Creature with Few Enemies

Seahorses have few enemies. They are too hard to find, and they are not very meaty. Still, seahorses sometimes turn up in the bellies of big fish, crabs, seabirds, and penguins.

Old-time Chinese medicine uses seahorses. And seahorses are popular for home aquariums. This means that seahorses are at risk from loss of habitat, storms, and too much collecting.

Glossary

camouflage (CAM oh flahj) — the ability of an animal to use colors, actions, and shapes to blend into its surroundings

crustaceans (crus TAY shunz) — a large group of related, boneless animals whose bodies are in sections, such as crabs, lobsters, and shrimp

dorsal (DOOR sul) — having to do with the back, such as the dorsal fin on a fish's back

flexes (FLECKS ez) — back and forth movements of a muscle or other body part

marine (meh REEN) — from or having to do with the sea

predators (PRED eh torz) — animals that hunt other animals for food

prey (PRAY) — an animal hunted by other animals

Index

Further Reading

Indiviglio, Frank. *Seahorses.* Barron's Educational Series, 2001
Miller, Sara Swan. *Seahorses, Pipefishes, and Their Kin.* Grolier, 2001
Walker, Sally M. *Sea Horses.* Carolrhoda Books, 1999

Websites To Visit

Seahorse Page: http://ourworld.compuserve.com/homepages/BMLSS/Seahors3.htm
    Pacific Seahorse:
http://www.oceanoasis.org/fieldguide/hipp-ing.html/
   Project Seahorse: http://www.seahorse.mcgill.ca/faq.htm

About The Author

Lynn Stone is the author of more than 400 children's nonfiction books. He is a talented natural history photographer as well. Lynn, a former teacher, travels worldwide to photograph wildlife in its natural habitat.